I0441610

ARMA

GOOD APPLICATION

Makes a Good Roof Better

A Simplified Guide:
Installing Laminated Asphalt Shingles
for Maximum Life & Weather Protection

Copyright © 2016, 2002, 1999, 1986, 1985 Asphalt
Roofing Manufacturers Association.

All rights reserved. No part of this book may be reproduced, stored, or
transmitted by any means—whether auditory, graphic, mechanical, or
electronic—without written permission of both publisher and author, except
in the case of brief excerpts used in critical articles and reviews. Unauthorized
reproduction of any part of this work is illegal and is punishable by law.

ARMA acknowledges and appreciates the assistance of the ARMA Steep
Slope Committee, and its editorial task force: Paul Casseri, Atlas Roofing;
Richard Snyder, CertainTeed Corporation; Bill Woodring, GAF; Don Shaw,
IKO Production, Inc.; Eileen Dutton, Malarkey Roofing; John Kouba,
Malarkey Roofing; Greg Keeler, Owens Corning; Sid Dinwiddie, PABCO
Roofing Products; Aaron Phillips, TAMKO Building Products, Inc.

ISBN: 978-1-4834-4656-1 (sc)
ISBN: 978-1-4834-4657-8 (e)

Because of the dynamic nature of the Internet, any web addresses or
links contained in this book may have changed since publication and
may no longer be valid. The views expressed in this work are solely those
of the author and do not necessarily reflect the views of the publisher,
and the publisher hereby disclaims any responsibility for them.

Any people depicted in stock imagery provided by Thinkstock are models,
and such images are being used for illustrative purposes only.
Certain stock imagery © Thinkstock.

Lulu Publishing Services rev. date: 03/14/2016

Contents

Foreword vii

Key Points for Shingle Selection 1
Key Points for Shingle Application 3
Preparations for New-Roof Construction 6
    Ensure Adequate Ventilation 6
    Prepare the Roof Deck 7
    Install Drip Edge 7
    Eaves Flashing for Ice Dam and Back-Up Protection 8
    Install the Underlayment 9
    Prepare Valley Flashings 11
Installing Shingles with New-Roof Construction 13
    Use Proper Nails & Nailing Methods 13
    Where to Begin 15
    The Starter Strip 15
    Applying the Shingles 18
    Applying Shingles at Valleys 18
    Flashings 20
    Hips and Ridges 25
Special Procedures for Low-Slope and
    Steep-Slope Roofs 26
    Low-Slope Roofs 26
    Steep-Slope Roofs 27

Reroofing via Roof Replacement or Roof Recover 29

Preparations for Reroofing 31

    Deck...31

    Underlayment...31

    Eaves Flashing (If Needed)...........................31

    Drip Edges..32

    Smoothing the Surface Prior to Recovering..............32

    Additional Information...............................32

Installing Shingles during Reroofing 33

    Installing Laminated Shingles Over Existing 3-Tab

       Shingles during a Roof Recover 33

    Flashings and Reroofing 34

    Hips and Ridges.....................................35

What Good Application Means to You...............36

About the Author 39

Foreword

This brochure was prepared by the Asphalt Roofing Manufacturers Association (ARMA) as a general guide for the installation of laminated asphalt roofing shingles. Laminated shingles contain more than one layer of material to create extra thickness. Laminated shingles may also be called "architectural" shingles or "three dimensional" shingles.

For more detailed information on the installation of asphalt shingles and other types of asphalt roofing products, refer to the *ARMA Residential Asphalt Roofing Manual,* which can be ordered on ARMA's website: www.asphaltroofing.org.

IMPORTANT

Every type of asphalt roofing product has its own application requirements and use specifications; always follow the product manufacturer's application instructions to help ensure proper installation. Before undertaking any roofing project, be sure to research and comply with all building codes and other laws and regulations that may apply to your particular situation.

DISCLAIMER: ARMA assumes and undertakes no responsibility for any liability, economic or other loss, or injury or damage to persons or property that may result from the use of the information contained in this brochure or from the purchase, application, installation, or other use of roofing materials.

WARNING: It is dangerous to walk, climb or work on a roof. To help avoid injury or death, exercise extreme care and follow all applicable safety precautions and procedures, including but not limited to applicable building code requirements and manufacturer's instructions, labels, and warnings.

Key Points for Shingle Selection

Roof Slope

The slope of your roof is determined by the vertical "rise" in inches for every horizontal twelve-inch (12") length (called the "run"). It is expressed with the rise mentioned first and the run mentioned second. For instance, if your roof has a four-inch (4") rise for every horizontal foot, then it is said to have a 4" in 12" slope (4:12).

A fairly easy way to determine the slope is to use a 12" carpenter's level. Set one end on the roof surface and level the carpenter's level. Using a tape measure or a ruler, measure from the other end of the 12" carpenter's level down to the roof surface. There are also free applications available for smartphones that include a slope indicator that may be used.

Color, Texture, Design & Exposure

Laminated asphalt shingles are available in a wide array of colors, textures, patterns, shapes, and dimensional depths to achieve an exceptionally broad range of aesthetic effects, and to complement most architectural styles.

"Exposure" is that portion of the shingle bared to the weather once installation is complete. The recommended exposure of a shingle creates its intended appearance and design pattern. In addition, the offset from course to course may affect the appearance of the finished roof. Always follow the specified manufacturer's application instructions carefully.

Fire and Wind Resistance

Most building codes require that roofing materials conform to certain fire-resistance standards. Asphalt shingles carry a Class A, Class B, or Class C fire classification, as defined by the ASTM E108/UL790 Standards, which set forth required fire tests of roof coverings. Class A rated products meet the most stringent fire-resistance criteria.

All ARMA member roofing manufacturers submit their products to third-party laboratories for testing to ensure that they conform to the requirements of ASTM's/UL's fire-resistance standards. Asphalt shingles which have been independently tested and shown to conform to these criteria carry a label on their packaging indicating Class A, B, or C fire-resistance classification.

Shingles also provide wind protection for roofs, typically through the use of a factory-applied sealant. The primary North American standards for measuring wind resistance of asphalt shingles are ASTM D7158 and ASTM D3161. Most building codes require asphalt shingles to be tested by a third-party laboratory and to carry a label certifying their wind resistance classification.

Key Points for Shingle Application

IMPORTANT – Follow the Shingle Manufacturer's Application Instructions and Ensure Compliance with Local Building Codes

Do not assume all shingles (or their application procedures) are the same. This is especially true of laminated shingles. To get the best performance and best appearance from any roofing product, read and follow all directions and specifications supplied by the manufacturer. To do otherwise may result in improper application, which could reduce or compromise roof performance and may affect the manufacturer's limited warranty.

Deck Preparation

A good roof requires that the entire roof structure be sound. The underlying structure should provide a rigid deck surface that will not sag, shift, or deflect under the weight of expected live or dead loads. Roof deck materials must be properly installed and free from excessive warps, knots, or resinous areas. The type, grade, thickness, and installation of roof decking materials should conform to all building code requirements.

Drainage

The primary function of a roof is to shed water. This involves not only the main roof surface, but also all of the junctions and breaks created by valleys, gables, wings, dormers, chimneys, vents, etc. Such breaks are protected by flashings, and great care must be exercised to make all flashings watertight and water-shedding. Corrosion-resistant drip edges at the rakes and eaves and adequate gutter and downspout placement are necessary for proper drainage.

Ventilation

Proper ventilation allows air to circulate freely under the roof deck to reduce roof surface temperatures and to carry away water vapor before it can condense. Many complaints of apparent roof leakage and /or deck rot are actually due to condensation from inadequate ventilation. Condensation can most often be eliminated with sufficient ventilation in the attic space or under-roof area, along with proper use of vapor-retarders when needed. The code-required minimum amount of ventilation for typical attic spaces is one square foot of unrestricted airflow for each 150 square feet of attic floor space.

Proper Nails and Nailing

Applying a good roof requires the use of proper nails and nailing techniques. Choosing the correct nails and applying them in the proper places with the appropriate methods will help to ensure a sound roof installation. Nails should be corrosion resistant, such as galvanized steel, stainless steel, or aluminum nails, and have a nominal shank diameter of 12 gauge and a minimumhead diameter of 3/8". IMPORTANT – Follow the shingle manufacturer's application instructions. Many shingles have special requirements regarding minimum nail length, nailing location, and number of nails per shingle.

On-Site Storage

Improper storage of asphalt roofing materials before installation can jeopardize the performance of the roof. Provisions must be made to protect roofing materials on site from undue water, cold, heat, and other weather-related exposures prior to application.

Preparations for New-Roof Construction

Ensure Adequate Ventilation

Adequate ventilation and air circulation can help ensure the elimination of unwanted humidity and condensation. If air is unable to circulate freely under a roof deck, moisture from cooking, bathing, and other sources inside the structure will condense upon reaching the colder roof sheathing. High humidity and moisture accumulation can lead to mold growth and deterioration of the roof's structural system and its component materials.

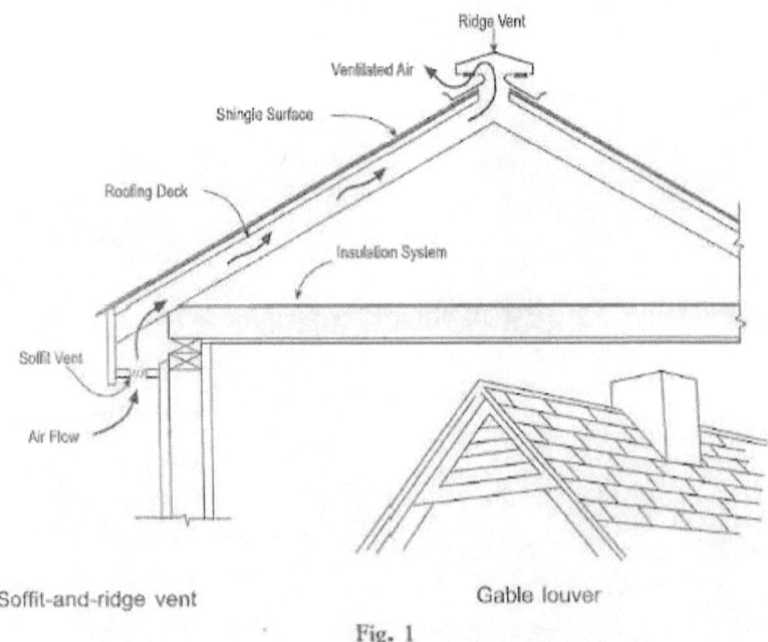

Soffit-and-ridge vent   Gable louver

Fig. 1

Most building codes require a minimum ventilation ratio of 1 sq. ft. net ventilating area per 150 sq. ft. of attic floor space (1:150). This may be achieved by the proper installation of sufficiently sized gable louvers or exhaust vents high on the roof. When approximately half of the vents are located at eaves or soffits, and the other half near the roof's peak or along the ridge for maximum airflow, free vent area can often be further reduced (minimum 1:300). Vents and louvers should remain open in all seasons and be free from any obstructions that may inhibit airflow.

Always verify that the roof's ventilation area meets minimum code requirements before installing shingles. For more information on ventilation practices, refer to the ARMA *Residential Asphalt Roofing Manual.*

Prepare the Roof Deck

The first step to a good roofing job lies with a proper roof deck. The deck should be built with structural-rated sheathing panels or equivalent non-veneer structural panels approved for such usage by an independent, third-party testing lab or agency. Actual type, grade, thickness, and installation techniques must conform to all building code requirements and manufacturer recommendations.

Install Drip Edge

A drip edge should be installed along the eaves and the rakes for efficient water-shedding at the roof's edges. It should be made of a corrosion-resistant material, and should extend a minimum 2" back from the roof edge and bend downward over the fascia (see Fig.2).

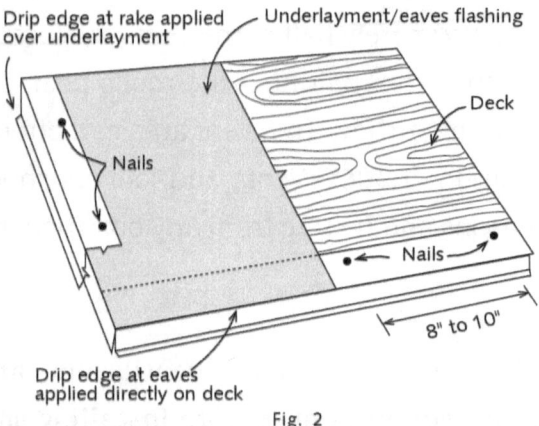

Fig. 2

Eaves Flashing for Ice Dam and Back-Up Protection

In climates where icing along the eaves is anticipated, eaves flashing should be installed to ensure maximum protection against possible damage from the back-up of water or slush in the eave trough due to ice dam formation. Eaves flashing may also be advisable in valleys, around dormers, above skylights, or in areas where the accumulation of leaves, pine needles, etc. in the eaves troughs may cause water back-up.

To install eaves flashing, a strip of self-adhering underlayment that complies with ASTM Standard D1970 should be applied directly to the deck. Underlayment width should be enough to extend up the roof from the eaves to a point at least 24" inside the interior wall line. If the underlayment is not wide enough to reach that point, install an additional course(s) of underlayment, overlapping the previous course as specified by the manufacturer (see Fig. 3). For additional protection in areas with heavy snow accumulation, it may be necessary to extend the underlayment to a point 36" or more inside the wall line.

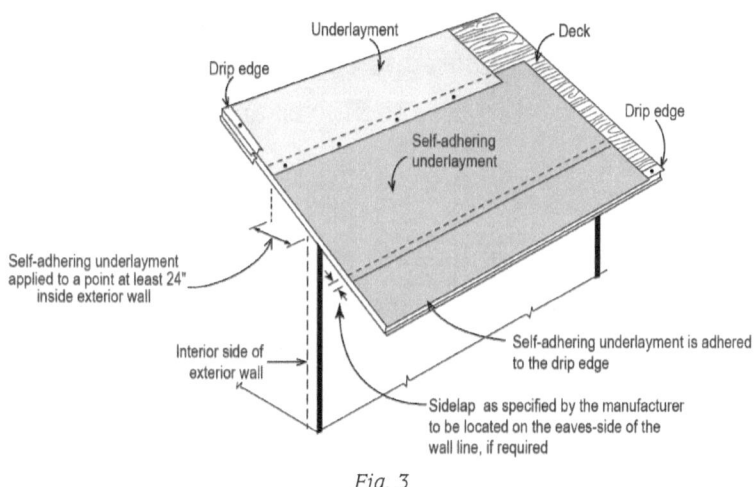

Fig. 3

Note: Because most self-adhering underlayments are vapor retarders, they should not be used beyond the recommended area without extra attention to attic ventilation. Be sure to follow the manufacturer's application instructions when using self-adhering underlayment.

Install the Underlayment

After the deck has been properly prepared and is dry, it should be covered with an appropriate asphalt-saturated underlayment felt that complies with ASTM D226, ASTM D4869, ASTM D6757, an alternative material recognized in a code compliance evaluation report, or as approved by the shingle manufacturer. Some local codes require specific underlayments.

If there are valleys, run a minimum 36" wide strip of underlayment centered on each valley, and secure 1" from felt edges with only enough nails to hold in place (see Fig. 4a). If two or more strips of underlayment are required to cover the entire valley length, lap the upper piece 12" over the lower and bond with asphalt roofing cement.

With valley underlayments in place, begin installing the horizontal courses of underlayment felt parallel to the eaves, lapping each course at least 2" over the underlying course, in accordance with the manufacturer's application instructions (see Fig. 4b). Secure the felt with only enough nails needed to hold it in place. If two or more pieces are required to continue a course, lap the ends at least 4".

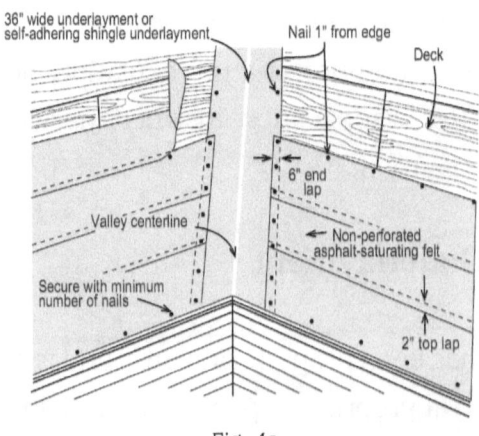

Fig. 4a

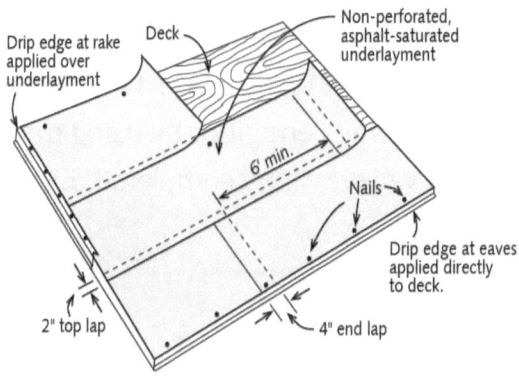

Fig. 4b

End laps in a succeeding course should be located at least 6 feet from the end laps of the preceding course. Extend the felt a minimum of 6" over hips and ridges. Where the roof meets a vertical surface, carry the underlayment at least 4" up the surface. After installing the underlayment, cover with shingles as soon as practical. IMPORTANT – Follow shingle manufacturer's application instructions. There are valley instructions specific to some products (e.g. open valleys required, self-adhering underlayment required).

Prepare Valley Flashings

To ensure proper drainage and prevent water leakage along the valley joints, valley flashing is required. This procedure is a typical valley flashing preparation. The manufacturer's application instructions may require alternate methods. Center a minimum 36" wide strip of roll roofing (50# or heavier) or a strip of self-adhering underlayment that complies with ASTM D1970 over the valley underlayment and secure 1" from edges with only enough nails to hold it in place (see Fig. 5). If two or more strips of roll roofing are required to cover the entire length of the valley, lap the upper piece 12" over the lower, and bond with asphalt roofing cement or by using the self-adhering underlayment. The valley will be completed during shingling.

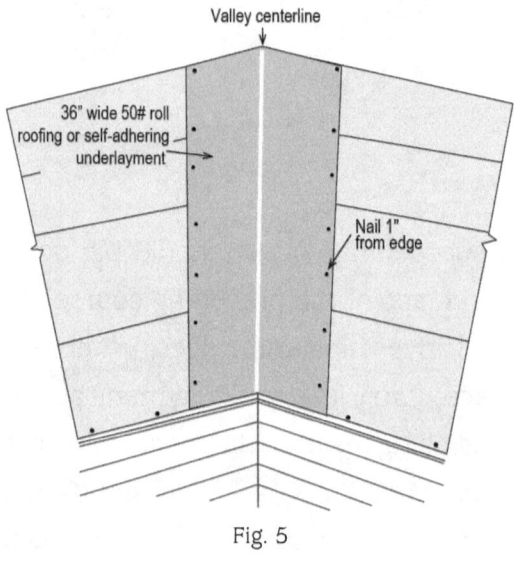

Fig. 5

Installing Shingles with New-Roof Construction

Use Proper Nails & Nailing Methods

Corrosion-resistant roofing nails should be used when affixing asphalt shingles. These nails should have a minimum nominal shank diameter of 12 gauge (0.105") and a minimum head diameter of 3/8".

Smooth- or rough-shanked nails are acceptable. Galvanized and aluminum nails generally have adequate corrosion resistance. Stainless steel nails are corrosion resistant. Nails shall be long enough to penetrate through the roofing materials and a minimum of 3/4" into the roof deck. Where the deck is less than 3/4" thick, the nail shall penetrate through the roof deck.

Drive nails straight and flush with the shingle surface; do not break the shingle surface with the nail head (Fig. 6). IMPORTANT – Follow the shingle manufacturer's application instructions regarding specified nail type, size, and grade, as well as special nailing procedures and proper positioning of nails on the shingle.

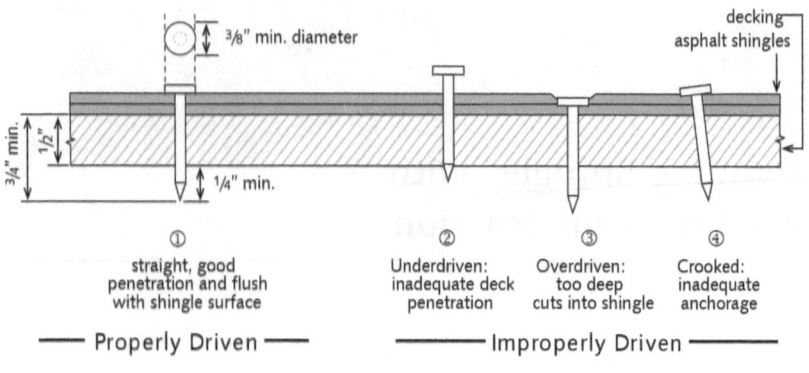

① straight, good penetration and flush with shingle surface

② Underdriven: inadequate deck penetration

③ Overdriven: too deep cuts into shingle

④ Crooked: inadequate anchorage

—— Properly Driven ——   ——— Improperly Driven ———

Fig. 6

If a nail does not penetrate the deck properly and cannot be tapped down into position, remove the nail, repair the hole with asphalt roofing cement that complies with ASTM D4586, and place another nail nearby. If necessary, replace the shingle.

With laminated shingles, follow the manufacturer's application instructions. Use a minimum of four nails per shingle (See Fig. 7a.). Always keep the shingle end joints of succeeding courses at least 2" away from the nails in the previous course. NAIL PLACEMENT IS CRITICAL. The manufacturer's application instructions must be followed for the number and placement of the nails. The nails must be placed so they penetrate through all the layers of the shingle (see Fig. 7b). Please be sure to follow your local building codes.

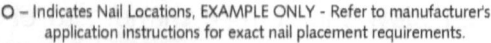

O – Indicates Nail Locations, EXAMPLE ONLY - Refer to manufacturer's application instructions for exact nail placement requirements.

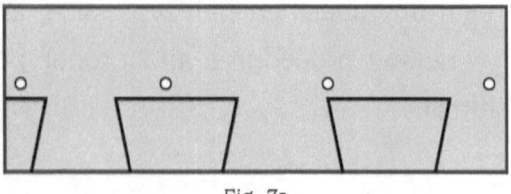

Fig. 7a

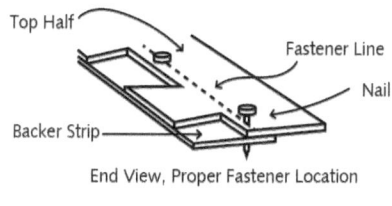

End View, Proper Fastener Location

Fig. 7b

Note: The examples in this booklet are for 5 5/8" exposure shingles. Although procedures for installing metric shingles are similar, be sure to follow all manufacturer application instructions.

Where to Begin

The use of horizontal and vertical chalk lines can assist in providing good shingle alignment. Because minor variations in shingle dimensions occasionally occur, chalk-line usage can help ensure the proper horizontal and vertical alignment, exposure and coverage of shingles.

If the roof surface is interrupted by a dormer or valley, begin applying shingles from a rake and work toward the break. If the surface is uninterrupted, begin at the rake deemed most visible. If both rakes seem equally visible, or it is a hipped roof, start at the center and work both ways.

The Starter Strip

The application of laminated asphalt shingles begins with a starter course (composed of "starter strips") to back up and fill in the spaces under the shingle end joints of the first course of shingles (see Fig. 8).

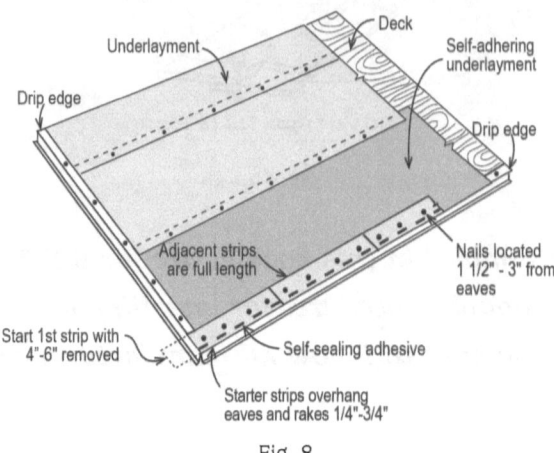

Fig. 8

If recommended by the laminated shingle manufacturer, self-sealing strip shingles of the same horizontal width and vertical exposure as the laminated shingles that are to be installed can be modified for use as starter strips by removing and discarding the exposed portion of each strip shingle and positioning the remaining piece along the eaves, with the factory-applied adhesive facing up and close to the eave's edge. Consult with the laminated shingle manufacturer for alternative starter strip options, some of which may be factory-made.

The starter course should overhang the eaves and rake edges by ¼" to ¾". If the drip edge extends out from the eaves and rake edges by ¼" to ¾", the shingles can be applied flush with the drip edge. **Manufacturers may require different starter strip techniques or provide starter strip materials that require specific application instructions. Follow the manufacturer's application instructions.**

Proper application of the first course of shingles is the most critical. Be sure it is laid out perfectly straight; check against the chalk lines to ensure proper alignment of subsequent courses. Shingles should be installed so that shingle ends are offset. The first course typically starts with a full shingle, but individual laminated shingles will have specific instructions for beginning the course of shingles. Generally, shingle ends should be offset from the course above and below by at least 4". Make sure that no end joint is less than 2" from any nail in an underlying course. Begin nailing from the end nearest the shingle just laid and proceed across, aligning each shingle carefully.

For best appearance and shingle function, the manufacturer's application instructions for shingle offsets and repeat pattern must be followed as indicated on the shingle wrapper. Each manufacturer has determined the optimum application pattern (for function and appearance) for each of their products. (See Fig. 9 as an example of one method.)

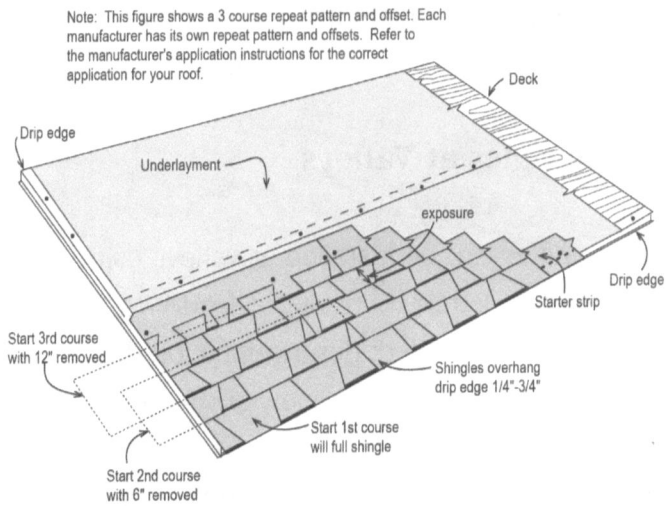

Fig. 9

Applying the Shingles

The first course starts with a full shingle, while succeeding courses start with progressively shorter pieces having portions removed according to the style of shingle being applied, until the application pattern repeats. By removing different amounts from the first shingle in each course, tabs in one course will not line up with those in the course below, creating the desired water resistant arrangement and attractive visual pattern.

For ease of illustration, a method using a non-specific offset dimension is shown in Fig. 9. For directions and illustration on appropriate methods, it is important to consult the manufacturer's application instructions.

With the 6" method, the first course begins with a full-length shingle. The second course begins with a shingle that is 6" shorter, and the third course starts with a shingle having 12" removed. The pattern repeats itself beginning with the fourth course, when a full-length shingle is used.

Applying Shingles at Valleys

Laminated shingles can be installed at valleys using the woven, open, or closed-cut method. Consult the *ARMA Residential Asphalt Roofing Manual* for detailed descriptions of these and other methods. The following is an overview of the closed-cut method.

Make sure the valley preparation is complete (see Figs. 4a and 5). Beginning with the lower-sloped roof plane, apply *only the first course* of shingles along the eaves, into and over the valley, with the last shingle extending at least 12" onto the intersecting roof and secured with two nails. Do not nail within 6" of the valley centerline. Never allow end-joints in the valley; add in a length of shingle so the end of the shingle extends at least 12" past the centerline.

Apply successive courses up the slope in the same manner, but to one roof plane only, starting with the lower-sloped roof. When the first plane is complete, snap a chalk line 2" from the valley centerline on the steeper-sloped side. Apply shingles to the steeper-sloped side, trimming the end shingles to the chalk line. Trim 1" on a 45-degree angle from the upper corner of all valley-abutting end shingles to direct water into the valley. Finally, embed the end of each end shingle in a 3" wide strip of asphalt roofing cement (see Fig.10).

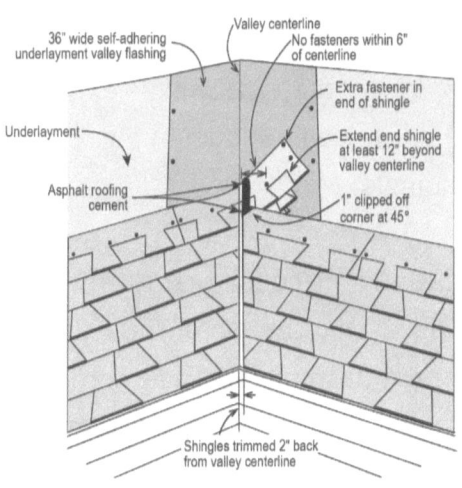

Fig. 10

Flashings

The following discussion is designed only to familiarize the reader with basic flashing concepts. For a more complete and detailed discussion of flashings and flashing application procedures, consult the *ARMA Residential Asphalt Roofing Manual.*

All intersecting roof planes and projections through the roof surface (vent stacks dormers, chimneys, etc.) require flashing to ensure these areas remain watertight. *Metal flashings should be of at least 26-gauge G-90 galvanized steel, 16 oz. copper or 0.025" aluminum.*

Flashing Against Vertical Sidewalls (Step Flashing)

Step flashing is used when a sloping roof plane meets a vertical surface. Typical step-flashing units are metal rectangles that are a minimum of 2" longer than the shingle exposure by 10" in size and that can be easily bent (shown in Fig. 11a as 7 5/8" for a 5 5/8" exposure shingle).

To install step flashing, place the first flashing unit over the end of the starter strip so that the tab of the end shingle in the first course will cover the flashing rectangle completely. Cement tab to flashing. Position the second step- flashing unit over the end shingle in the first course, above the butt, so the cemented tab of the end shingle in the second course will cover the flashing unit completely. Repeat. (See Fig. 11a and Fig. 11b).

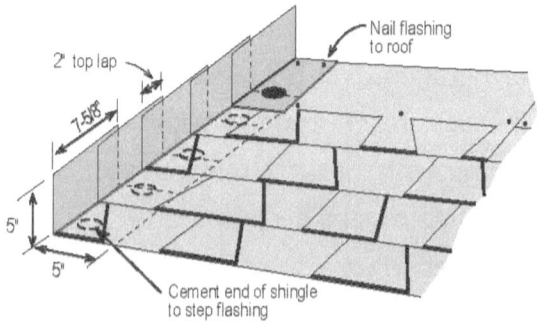

Fig. 11a

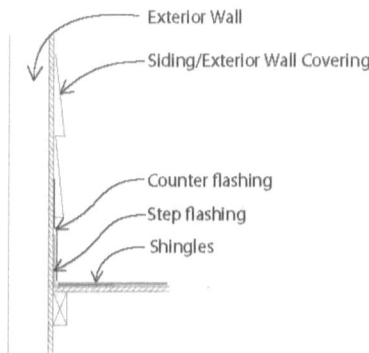

Fig. 11b

Bend each flashing unit to cover the roof deck by at least 5" and to run snugly up the wall surface for 5". Secure the flashing to the roof with one or two nails. Do not nail the flashing to the wall. To prevent leakage, the step flashing must then be counter-flashed.

Flashing around Chimneys

Proper flashing installed around chimneys is a critical and important component in achieving proper water diversion. The components attached to the deck and the masonry must be able to move independently without allowing water leakage. Chimney flashings generally require metal apron flashings secured to the roof deck and metal counter-flashings secured to the masonry. This allows the counter-flashing to move independently from the apron flashing without affecting water runoff. Crickets are recommended on chimneys over 24" wide, and are required by most building codes for chimneys over 30" wide. This section gives some basic details, but because of the wide variety of chimney details, the *ARMA Residential Asphalt Roofing Manual* should be consulted for further details.

Apron Flashing at *Chimney Front:* Apply shingles up to the front edge of the chimney and apply a thin coat of ASTM D41 asphaltic primer to the chimney brickwork. Make and place a metal apron flashing over the shingles at the chimney front. Bend the wings flush with the chimney side and set in asphalt roofing cement. The flashing should extend at least 4" over the shingles and 12" up the vertical face of the chimney (see Fig. 12).

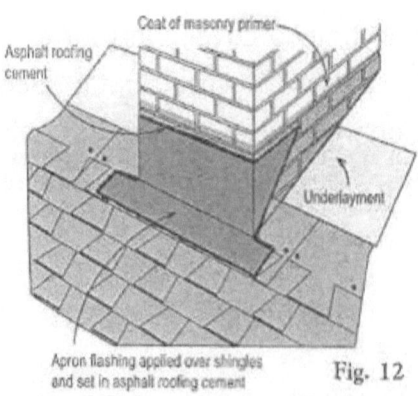

Coat of masonry primer

Asphalt roofing cement

Underlayment

Apron flashing applied over shingles and set in asphalt roofing cement

Fig. 12

Step Flashing at Chimney Sides: Place metal step flashing on the chimney sides. Secure step flashing to the masonry with asphalt roofing cement and to the deck with nails. Embed the end shingles in asphalt roofing cement, overlapping the flashing.

Flashing the Cricket: Place metal flashing over the cricket and back of the chimney, cutting and bending the metal flashing to cover the cricket and extend onto both the roof surface and up the brickwork by at least 6", and far enough laterally (2" minimum) to lap the step flashing on the sides. Cut another flashing strip to fit over the ridge of the cricket and extend onto the roof at the back of the cricket by at least 6". Bring the end shingles up to the cricket and cement in place (see Fig. 13).

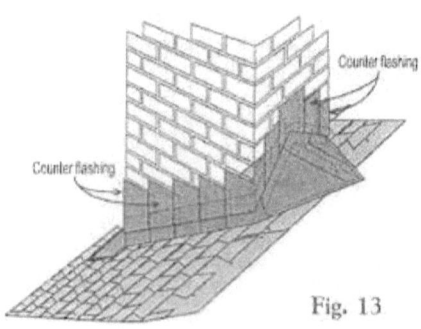

Fig. 13

Chimney Counter-Flashings: Place counter-flashing over all apron, cricket and step flashings. Set into brickwork by raking out a mortar joint to a depth of 1 ½" and inserting the bent edge of the counter-flashing into the cleared joint. Refill the joint with Portland cement mortar and bend the counter-flashing down to snugly cover the step flashing. Use a continuous piece of counter-flashing at the chimney front; use uniform pieces at the sides to match the brick joint and roof pitch, starting at the lowest point and overlap each by at least 3".

NOTE: Chimney flashings are complex so please refer to the *ARMA Residential Asphalt Roofing Manual* for complete details.

Flashings around Stacks and Vent Pipes

Apply shingles up to the pipe. Cut a hole in a shingle to fit over the pipe, and set the shingle in asphalt roofing cement. Place a preformed flashing flange snugly over the pipe and set in asphalt roofing cement. Resume applying shingles, cutting them to fit around the pipe, and embedding them in asphalt roofing cement where they overlay the flange. Avoid excessive use of cement, which can cause blistering. Do not drive nails close to the pipe. When completed, the lower part of the flange will overlap the lower shingles, while the upper and side shingles will overlap the flange (Fig. 14).

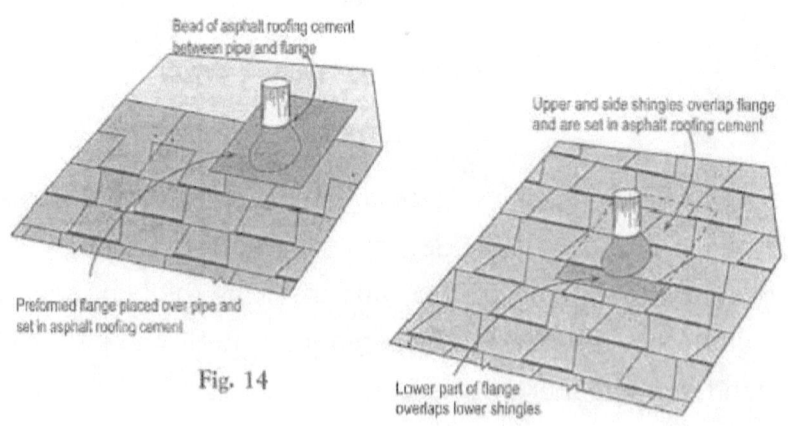

Bead of asphalt roofing cement between pipe and flange

Preformed flange placed over pipe and set in asphalt roofing cement

Fig. 14

Upper and side shingles overlap flange and are set in asphalt roofing cement

Lower part of flange overlaps lower shingles

Hips and Ridges

Apply shingles up to the hip or ridge from both sides, adjusting the last few courses so that the ridge capping will adequately cover the top courses of shingles equally on both sides of the ridge.

If a manufacturer has supplied special hip and ridge shingles, install per instructions. Hip and ridge shingles may also be made from three-tab shingles. As three-tab shingles come in many sizes, cut the shingles down through the tab cutouts on three-tab shingles or to a minimum of 9" x 12" on two-tab, four-tab or no-cutout shingles. For a neat application, taper the headlap portion of each cap shingle slightly so that it is narrower than the exposed portion. Apply by bending each along its centerline to extend equally on either side of the hip or ridge, giving a 5" exposure (Fig. 15). Secure with one nail on each side, 5 ½" back from the exposed end and 1" up from the edge. Use nails ¼" longer than those recommended for shingles. Begin applying hip shingles at the bottom of the hip. On ridges, begin at the end opposite the direction of prevailing winds. If a ridge vent is used, install ridge vent and capping shingles per manufacturer's application instructions.

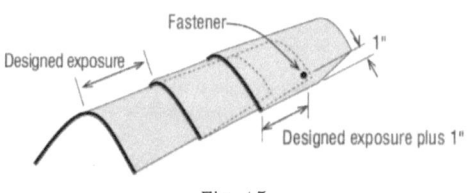

Fig. 15

Special Procedures for Low-Slope and Steep-Slope Roofs

Low-Slope Roofs

Laminated asphalt shingles may be used on low-slope roofs ranging from 2" to 4". Do not use laminated shingles on slopes less than 2" per foot. Check the manufacturer's application specifications that are printed on the shingle wrapper. Applications ranging from 2" to 4" are considered low-slope roofs and require special underlayment application practices.

Where allowed by the building code, the generally preferred practice on low-slope roofs is to cover the full deck with self-adhering underlayment that complies with ASTM D1970, applying the underlayment directly to the deck. Be sure to follow the manufacturer's application instructions when using self-adhering underlayment. Because most self-adhering underlayments are vapor retarders, confirm attic ventilation is adequate, balanced, and evenly distributed to assure proper airflow.

As an alternative practice, the "traditional" method of preparing a low-slope deck is to cover the deck with two layers of underlayment. Begin by placing and fastening a 19" wide underlayment starter course along the eaves. Place a full width sheet (36") over the starter course sheet with the long edge placed along the eaves and completely overlapping the underlayment starter course. All succeeding courses are 36" wide and should be positioned to overlap the preceding course by 19". Secure each course by using only enough fasteners to hold it in place until the shingles are applied. End laps should be 12" wide and located at least 6' from end laps in the preceding course.

Note: If the full width sheet of underlayment is not 36" wide, see the manufacturer's instructions for the correct overlap dimensions.

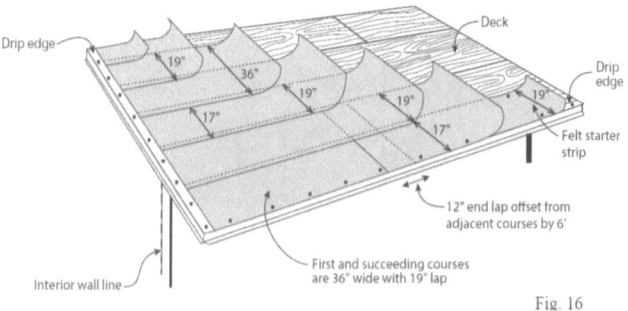

Fig. 16

Steep-Slope Roofs

Installation of shingles on roof slopes exceeding 21" per foot requires special application and fastening procedures. Upon installation of the shingles, immediately cement each shingle with four quarter-sized dabs of asphalt roofing cement or as recommended by the shingle manufacturer (see Fig. 17).

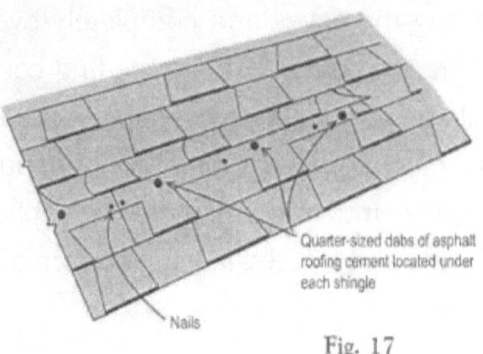

Fig. 17

Reroofing via Roof Replacement or Roof Recover

Overview

The first step in reroofing is to decide whether the existing roofing should remain in place or be removed. In general, roofs covered with asphalt shingles or asphalt roll roofing may be left in place. Local building codes often set the maximum number of roofs that may be installed before tear-off becomes mandatory.

Because the new roof will add weight to the structure, the roof framing must be strong enough to support this additional weight, as well as the weight of the roofers and their equipment. It is also important that the existing deck be in good condition so that it can provide adequate anchorage for the new roofing nails. Finally, if old roofing is warped, curled, or badly weathered – or if the underlying structure is deteriorated or damaged to the point where providing a sound, level surface is difficult – the existing roofing should be removed and the underlying deck and roof structure repaired or replaced as necessary.

Before reroofing, whether over an existing roof or with a tear-off situation, carefully inspect all adjacent areas of the building and make any necessary repairs to or replacements of deteriorating wood trim, chimney mortar joints, flashings, etc. Rebuild, replace, or reline and clean gutters and make sure there is adequate under-roof ventilation. After making all necessary repairs, clean all debris from the roof surface.

The following pages focus on the two most common reroofing situations: (1) roof replacement, in which asphalt shingles are applied where existing materials have been removed, and (2) roof recover, in which asphalt shingles are applied over existing asphalt shingles or asphalt roll roofing. For detailed instructions on the removal of old roofing and preparing for reroofing with asphalt shingles over a variety of existing roofing materials, refer to the *ARMA Residential Asphalt Roofing Manual.*

Preparations for Reroofing

Deck

When performing a roof replacement, the old roofing material must be removed as completely as possible down to the deck or, if previously installed, down to the self-adhering underlayment. Remove as much of the existing roofing as possible including fasteners, moving the debris out of the path of workers and sweeping all loose material off the roof. Extra care must be taken around chimneys and other roof penetrations. Replace any rotted or otherwise damaged roof sheathing. Remove or drive flush any remaining fasteners and sweep the deck surface clean a final time.

Underlayment

If the old roofing has been removed, cover the deck with new asphalt-saturated felt underlayment as for new construction. If the old asphalt shingles are to remain, no additional underlayment is generally required.

Eaves Flashing (If Needed)

If the old roofing has been removed, apply a self-adhering underlayment. If new shingles are being applied over the existing layer, a self-adhering underlayment is typically not required. If, however, there have been ice dam or leakage concerns with the old roof, it may be advisable to remove the old roofing, and reroof using a self-adhering underlayment as previously described.

Drip Edges

Remove any badly worn drip edges and replace with new ones (see Fig. 2).

Smoothing the Surface Prior to Recovering

If installing asphalt shingles over existing asphalt shingles, remove or nail down any loose, curled, lifted, or broken shingles. Replace missing shingles with new ones for an unbroken nailing base. Hammer down all loose or protruding nails or remove them and refasten the shingle. Remove all existing hip and ridge shingles.

Additional Information

For further information, refer to ARMA's Technical Bulletins that deal with reroofing:

- "Self-Adhering Underlayment Removal Prior to Steep Slope Reroofing"
- "Reroofing: Tear Off vs. Recover"

Installing Shingles during Reroofing

If the old roofing has been removed and new underlayment installed, shingle application is the same as that for new construction.

Installing Laminated Shingles Over Existing 3-Tab Shingles during a Roof Recover

If applying laminated shingles over existing three-tab asphalt shingles and both have the <u>same</u> exposure dimension (this will not occur often), then the "nesting procedure" can be used. Nesting minimizes the unevenness that might result from the new shingles bridging over the butts of the old shingles.

If new shingles are of a different exposure than existing shingles, then the existing shingles should be torn off before proceeding. Directly applying shingles over uneven surfaces can cause the new shingles to deform, negatively affecting finished appearance and preventing the sealant from activating properly, thus decreasing wind resistance. It is not recommended to install laminated asphalt shingles directly over existing laminated shingles of *any* exposure dimension due to the unevenness of the existing multi-layered shingles. In addition, if shingles are cut down in size in an attempt to "nest" into place, the sealant may shift away from the lowermost edge of the shingle, thus decreasing wind resistance.

Flashings and Reroofing

If the old roofing has been removed, flashing procedures for reroofing generally follow those outlined for new construction. If the old shingles are left in place when reroofing, some flashing application details may be different. Flashings in good condition may be left in place and reused. The following are general guidelines regarding flashings when reroofing over existing asphalt shingles. For specific instructions and illustrations, consult the *ARMA Residential Asphalt Roofing Manual.*

Valley Flashings: If the existing roof has an open valley, build up the exposed area of the valley with a mineral-surfaced roll roofing product to a level flush with the existing roofing. Then install new open valley flashing in the same manner as for new construction, overlapping the existing shingles. The preferred treatment, however, is to construct an open or closed-cut valley with the new shingles crossing over the valley filler strip.

Vertical Sidewall Flashings: Trim the new end shingles to within ¼" of the existing step flashing. Embed the last 3" of the end shingle of each course in asphalt roofing cement. Also apply a bead of cement with a caulking gun at the joint between the shingle ends and the sidewall.

Vent Flashings: If the existing flashing is in good condition, lift the lower part of the flange and install new shingles beneath it. Secure the flange back in place with asphalt roofing cement and apply additional cement around the outside of the pipe to protect the joint between the pipe and flange. Resume shingle application, cutting shingles in successive courses to fit snugly around the pipe, and embedding them in asphalt roofing cement.

Chimney Flashings: If the existing flashings are in good condition, lift the lower part of the front base flashing and install new shingles beneath. Cover the area under the flashing with asphalt roofing cement and set the flashing back in place. At the chimney sides, trim the new shingles to within ¼" of the existing step flashing, and embed the last 3" of each end shingle in a thin layer of asphalt roofing cement. Apply a bead of cement with caulking gun at the joint between the ends of the new shingles and the flashings. If the existing cricket flashing is metal, apply new shingles up to the flashing and set the last 3" of each end shingle in asphalt roofing cement.

Hips and Ridges

If the old roofing has been removed, apply new hip and ridge shingles as if for new construction. If reroofing over existing shingles, remove the old hip and ridge shingles and replace with new shingles, using the same methods as outlined for new construction.

What Good Application Means to You

If You're a Dealer...

Good application will enable the roofing products you sell to give the kind of performance for which you want to be known.

If You're An Applicator or Roofing Contractor...

Good application is good business. You want to be known as a builder of good roofs. You also want to reduce the chance and cost of callbacks.

If You're an Architect, Builder or Contractor...

People who buy your homes or your professional or contracting services expect lasting values. Extra minutes spent on a job to ensure good application may save hours and dollars later.

If You're a Homeowner...

You have to live under the roof. You want the best roof for your money.

Product Specification References

Shingles:
ASTM D3018
ASTM D3462
CSA A123.5

Underlayment:
ASTM D226
ASTM D4869
ASTM D6757
CSA A123.3

Self-Adhering Underlayment:
ASTM D1970
CSA A123.22

Asphalt Roofing Cement:
ASTM D4586

About the Author

The Asphalt Roofing Manufacturers Association (ARMA) is a trade association representing the majority of North America's asphalt roofing manufacturing companies, plus their raw material suppliers. The association includes almost 95 percent of the nation's manufacturers of bituminous-based roofing products.

www.ingramcontent.com/pod-product-compliance
Lightning Source LLC
Chambersburg PA
CBHW020906310526
45786CB00018B/1877